# TRAIL
*of My*
# TEARS

# TRAIL
## *of My*
# TEARS

*My Poetic Journey from*
*Ashes to Beauty*

## Keierra Moore

XULON PRESS

Xulon Press
2301 Lucien Way #415
Maitland, FL 32751
407.339.4217
www.xulonpress.com

Printed in the United States of America.

Paperback ISBN-13: 978-1-66281-355-9
Ebook ISBN-13: 978-1-66281-356-6

# DEDICATION

To my parents Keith and Florence Moore, rest in peace. I get my creativity from them. To all those who supported my dreams and to those who doubted me. I'd be just another hopeless case with you. I pray this book shows you a deeper side of me, but shows more importantly the truth. Some of the poems are letter style, more free verse, and some actually have stanzas. Embark on the journey with me down the trails of my tears to get to my never-ending smile. I dedicate this book to all the Dreamers and people who were told their plans did not matter. To all those who never fit in the box others tried to keep you in. I dedicate this to my children and their futures. For my brother J and his future. To Kecia, Ma Wendy, Ma Tiki, Ma Jeanette, Ma Tanya, Pa Pa Bill and his family. To my enemies and friends. I love you all! The sky is not the limit!!!

Keierra

# TABLE OF CONTENTS

# VOICE CRYING OUT

There's a voice crying out in the wilderness saying "repent, change your ways. The Kingdom of God is at hand."

A man washed people in water baptized them by faith in I AM. Preparing the way for the one who baptizes with fire.

There's a voice crying out in the wilderness
saying "repent, repent."

He looked rough but loved so truly.

Many followed him and waited to see the One greater his sandals their teacher said he was unworthy to touch.

There's a voice crying out in the wilderness in every nation using every language of the Earth.

# REWIND

Let me say this so it's clear and you can hear... my heart.

So much has happened this month took in someone thinking I could help she got me drowning in the depth... of sorrow.

It's my birthday and I'm sad missing my mom and my dad. Wishing someone could love me like Christ in the flesh of the male persuasion.

What do I do? I got to press rewind to go back in time and try it all over again. Things aren't what I hoped I struggle more than I'd like to people have great opinions but not a way out so what do I do? I got to press rewind to go back in time and try it all over again

# PROMISE RING

So, after work I hit up the mall.
I went in walking tall not feeling small at all.
I saw a ruby n crystal ring that spoke to me. I put it on to
see if it fit me. It did perfectly.

My promise ring gleamed and shined.
My promised ring showed me I must get things aligned.
I promised to seek first the Kingdom and God's will.

I promised to come out of self and living by what I feel.
I promised to cut off those who stress me out,
doesn't matter how long I've known u without a doubt.

I promised to provide for my boys and teach them respect.
I promised to love myself, stop with the self-neglect.
My promise ring gleamed and shined.
It showed me I had to get things aligned.

# BREAKFAST CLUB REVOLT

Tears in my oatmeal

sighs on my toast

screams in my orange juice

this is a breakfast club revolt...

# LETTER TO MY UNBORN

Dear Love,

This is your Mother. I am so excited to await your arrival. I played you some music today. It may have been kind of loud. Sorry about that baby. I will play more music for you as I get it. I hope you are growing strong, and healthy. Daddy is happy he gives you kisses all the time. Sometimes he makes me cry with things he says but don't worry he'll never do it to you. You are blessed. You will be used by God at a young age love so I hope you will be ready for that. It was prophesied that you will be a carrier of God's glory and have a testimony even in school. Mommy has to get on the right path. Your grandparents are looking down from Heaven at you and will be your guardian angels. I know if they were alive, they would love you and be as excited as I am. You will have four uncles no aunts at the moment love, but you will have a lot of cousins. That'll be really fun when you get older. Babe you really hurt my tummy sometimes but I guess that's okay because you need space to grow. I'm trying to find a place for us to live for after you are born, because daddy's mom Grandma said we may have to leave when you are born. I think that sucks but it'll be okay. I am going to dedicate you to God maybe when you are six weeks old. I will be done with New Member s class by then. I start college next spring. That may be Jan or Feb of next year. I will be doing it online. I should be done halfway by your second b day. I want to put you in private school but I have a long time to find a good one for you. I pray you haven't been starving or not sleeping. I am going to start reading you stories and the Bible so you can use to it. I love you so, so, so much baby and I cannot wait until you are born.

# MY SWEET ISHI

Lord you have
love everlasting
love everlasting
love everlasting

my heart my whole heart I give to you oh yes, I do. My
heart my whole heart is yours my King my sweet Ishi
you are everything I hoped for
everything I desired everything I needed
you are you are

Lord you have
love everlasting
love everlasting
love everlasting

my heart my whole heart is yours my King my
sweet Ishi

Lord you have
love everlasting
love everlasting
love everlasting

my sweet Ishi
Jesus

# I'VE DECIDED

I've decided to ask God to gather my soul.

I've decided to take a vow of celibacy and live Holy.

My flesh hurts when I say "No, I can't get with that"

But my spirit wanted to get on track.

I've decided to take control of my body and soul

I've decided to walk down that narrow road.

I've decided to look my sexuality in the face

And you know what she laughed said I'll never give it up

I've decided to scream "Enough is enough!"

I've always felt like living holy was though that's
because I was faking it

I've decided God is worth the realness of my
flesh bowing in totally submission!

So all the guys who want to be mad it's you who I am
dismissing!

I've decided to give God the glory with my
mind, soul, and my body

I've decided to go in the inner courts, holy of holy's
not the lobby

I've decided God should have all of me not just one part

I've decided it's time I give Him my whole heart!

Now people condemn me because I'm pregnant now

But I know for a fact that My God can turn any situa-
tion around!

To those who laugh "He who is without sin,
let him cast the first stone"

# OVERFLOW

fill me to overflow
over flow
over flow of you
oh Lord an overflow
of You

fill me to overflow
over flow
an overflow of you

my heart is aching it feels
like its breaking
fill my cracked spaces my
hidden places with You

oh oh overflow
an overflow of you

my hearts cry...

# ALLEGIANCE

Have you ever thought about what that word really means? As children we have said it in America every start of the school day when we recited the pledge.

The Webster's dictionary defines *Allegiance* as *1.The obligation of a feudal vassal to his liege lord. 2.Devotion or loyalty to a person, group or cause.*

Do you have a *"lord"*? A lord can be a king or queen you honor. Or your significant other if you like that. It can be anything we chose to have control over us.

In my past I pledged my allegiance to people, my government, and money. Think about if you have too.

Now that I am older my allegiance is to our Creator. The Highest One. The Righteous King. Immanuel. Great I AM. Have you met Him?

He was there when you were formed in your mother's womb. He was there when you had your first heart break. He was there when you were ready to give up! Our Creator is ALWAYS with us.

I ask you to close your eyes after reading this and speak out loud "Are You there?" And wait to hear from Him. He longs to hear your voice. He loves you with an ever-lasting love.

(NIRV) *"God so loved the world that he gave his one and only Son. Anyone who believes in him will not die but will have eternal life."*

Peace and blessings be unto you.

# SEEING IS NOT BELIEVING

Have you ever heard the saying *"Seeing is believing?"*

I am certain that you have. What did it mean? What you see is truth maybe. Or if you can see it must be real.

The Word of God tells us to **walk by faith and not by sight.** Yet many of us are led by what we see. I myself was trying to fit the beauty mode that the world said I should fit. I can tell you here and now that I stopped that mess. I was being lied too by the masses of hurt people who are in competition with each other and aren't comfortable with themselves. I am now because I believe what 2 Corinthians 5:17 says. The NLT version says *"This means that anyone who belongs to Christ has become a new person. The old life is gone; a new life has begun!"*

Bless Jesus. I don't have to care about what I see. I am a mom of four beautiful bouncing boys! That six pack is doable but not going to be the death of me. And my 21-year-old used van is getting us where we need to be. I have no need to keep up with the Jones's nor Kardashian's. Proverbs 31 says that **beauty is fleeting but a woman who pleases the LORD shall be praised.**

Looks can be deceiving. Ambition can kill your spirit. Make your heart sick. And if you are not getting wisdom or understanding in all that getting then what is the use? Seeing is NOT believing because the lust of the eyes is just that lust. Lust is defined as a deep longing for something; addictive yearning. If that is ruling your life it can also ruin it.

Remember the Word says what good is it to gain the whole world and lose your soul!

Be blessed!

# WILL THE REAL SONS OF GOD PLEASE STAND UP?

"Will the REAL sons of God please stand up?" That is what I am asking. We as children of the Most High God are to be in the world but not of the world. Are we truly different?

Let's see. Does your church building have a place for single parents and the elderly? Does if over an outreach program to help with the needs you may have? How about life skills that teach you how to treat people how you'd like to be treated? If not maybe we all can learn a thing or two from reading the book of Acts and 1&2 Timothy.

I hear a lot "there is no perfect church". Yet perfect in the Greek meant complete or whole not the same as in English. So, as you just learned by reading my previous post (What is the church?) You are alone complete and whole in Christ.

If Christ is not the foundation then everything fails! Thus, the reason why the real children of God need to rise up in the Earth. We need to fight the good fight of faith and overtake and recover all the enemy has stolen! We need to set spiritual captives free! We need to declare "Thy Kingdom come, that will be done on Earth as it is in Heaven."

Arise, arise and put-on strength!

# WHAT IS CHURCH?

When you read the title of this you may have thought a place where believers gather weekly to worship. Or a place to experience the presence of God. Those are good but not totally correct.

Don't kill the messenger. Please hear me out. The word of God says to us in Corinthians that our body is the temple of the Holy Spirit. Later in the Holy book it says where two or more are gathered in my name there I am in the midst. I being the Most High God in the statement. Christ told us that if we abide in Him, while He is in the Father then the Father abides in us. Also, we know that God is Love. And we should abide in Love.

So, church in the book of Acts was a house or hidden place where believers ate a meal, sang praise to God and did miracles. Shoot even a jail was church. Sadly, America and other nations have lost sight of what church really is and should be. It has become a "charitable organization" ran by "donations" and faith. An agency of sorts. I would say to them in leadership as Christ Jesus did "He that hath an ear let him hear what the Spirit of the Lord is saying…" Come back to your first love. We are the body of Christ! No group of people are more worthy of the name "children of God" than the next. He came for the Jew and Gentile.

If you have opened the door to Christ Jesus then you are His Church. His Holy Spirit will lead and guide you into all truth. Let us not forget that "The truth shall set us free"!

Peace be unto you!

# A NEW THING

Isaiah Chapter 43 and verse 19, starts off with God saying, "Behold, I will do a new thing;".

I want to pray for this to come to pass in your life and in the lives of everyone around you.

Holy Father, Our Abba,

I say thank You for waking us up this morning. This is your day You have given us, help us to rejoice and be glad in it. You said in Your Living Word that You will do a NEW THING. Help us to accept the new thing, help us to accept the newness of life in Jesus Christ's name. Bring us to full and total oneness with You through Your Holy Spirit within us. Draw Your creation back unto You O King of kings. Let Your love be poured out in this hour. Let Your glory be revealed in us. We want to magnify You O our Redeemer. Unify us for Your plans and purposes. Teach us to love our neighbors as ourselves. Teach us to love our enemies. Help us to LET GO of the PAST. Cover us Abba, under the shadow of Your wings like in Psalm 91. Have Your way in this day and forever in Christ Jesus' name we pray Amen and Amen.

# LOVE

Did you know that Love is ALIVE?

Did you know that it is needed MORE THAN EVER BEFORE?

Did you know that there is NO LIMIT to it? No? Well now you do.

I know you may have used this word before or heard it countless times but I beg you today to only say it when you mean it. I implore you to use love as a shield, as a bridge, and a banner.

Love those who look different than you.

Love those who can barely speak English.

Love those who are not politically correct.

Love those who are poor.

Love those who are rich.

Love those who are uneducated.

Love those who are educated.

Love those who deserve it.

Love those who do not deserve it.

Love in action and in deed.

Love your neighbor, whether white, "blue", black, yellow, brown, or red as yourself.

Love covers a multitude of sin.

Love holds NO RECORD of WRONGS.

Love ENDURES ALL THINGS.

Love one another as Christ Jesus LOVES US!

# AMOUR

**Amour** means love

**Love** means so much

sacrifice

patience

L-O-V-E

**Amour** means love

**Love** means so much

# TRUTH

Teach me

Really allow me to

Understand

The

Holy One

#micropoetry #acrostic #Jesus #Christ #faith #goals

# YOU GOT THIS!

Do me a favor, take a deep breath. Hold it for a few seconds, now breathe out. Do it twice more. You feel more relaxed? Good. Take a moment to stop and ponder on the truth. You are alive. Someone did not wake up this morning. Smile and be thankful for that. I have experienced so much hardship in my life. I should have been dead and gone but God had a plan for me. He has a plan for you. You may not believe in God or Jesus Christ, but He believes in you. Your life was His will. Yes, your parents had something to do with it too, but ultimately it was ALL Him.

You were created by the UNIVERSE'S GREATEST CREATOR! The GREATEST ARTIST OF ALL TIME! That should bring a smile to your face. You ARE NOT A MISTAKE! You were formed, molded and shaped into the beautiful or handsome image which is you for a purpose greater than you may know. I hope that while this year is coming to an end you find those who can speak positively into your life. Empty your circle of all the negative people who want you to fail. You can do NOTHING BUT WIN! So, throw your hands up, and let them stay there. Shout out to T-pain. Be inspired to become a better you than you were before. The best is yet to come!

I trust you can make the world a better place.

You just have to believe it.

You were created for great things! Go do them, go make them happen.

Nothing is too small. Nothing is impossible.

# EYES WIDE SHUT

She was beautiful
Compared to others
She was petite
But she was
POWERFUL!

Her eyes sparkled
They were big, intriguing,
Massively mysterious

She cannot see the Death
Knocking at her door
Or the bloodshed of innocents
She lives with her eyes wide shut!

She is a business guru
A networking Queen
She is pleasant and friendly

That is only a mirage
in the Oasis of
your mind

She truly is conniving and deceitful
She'd break every promise
To get ahead

Her eyes sparkled
They were big, intriguing,
Massively mysterious

She cannot see the Death
Knocking at her door
Or the bloodshed of innocents
She lives with her eyes wide shut!

Her first name is America
Her middle is Justice
Last name is Unity
But she dropped it
Like a celebrity

She kills her own children
And breaks down her own
Fortresses

She may never again be
*"Land of the brave, home of the free!"*

Death becomes her like
Ms. Goldie
And she cares not because
She's accustomed to
Walking blindly
Pride comes before the fall...
Even Rome was as Humpty Dumpty

Her eyes sparkled
They were big, intriguing,
Massively mysterious

She cannot see the Death
Knocking at her door
Or the bloodshed of innocents
She lives with her eyes wide shut!

Will she ever open them?

# STILL

I am sitting still

Lying down on the couch now

The world is still

Not quite quiet yet still

Moving steadily on

Not going anywhere

Be still

# M.E.R.C.Y

**Mercy Ever Reaching You**.

That is what mercy means for me.

The Most High God through Himself in the form of the Christ, sought me out until I was found.

I was lost doing things my own way.

The Bible says "There is a way that seems right unto a man but that way leads unto death."

Here I was being in control of my own destiny and leading myself to an early grave. If not physically then spiritually.

But MERCY called out my name and pursued end-lessly after me.

God help me to see the error in doing for myself and allowing others to.

He showed me that He will NEVER fail me or disown me.

He showed me what true love is. (Read 1 Corinthians 13). His love is all that plus more!

If MERCY has called your name answer. Even if you are reluctant do it anyway. He'd not stop drawing you back unto Himself.

Jeremiah 29:11 tells us "I know the plans I have for you says the LORD plans of good and not of evil. To give you a hope and a future." Christ in us is the hope of glory! Praise God! And the future is an everlasting life of abundance in Christ Jesus though the leading of the sweet Spirit of the Holy Ghost our Helper. He is with us always!

Let go of the reign of your life and give yourself to the One Wise God our Saviour. His mercy and love endure forever!

# ABOUT ME

I am a Daughter of Virtue. I child of the King of kings. I have always loved words since I was a little girl. I expressed my emotions through rhyme all the time. (See it happens even by accident) I know that other people enjoy poetry as much as I do and wanted to share my own gift with you! I hope you can relate to my work or at least are encouraged by it. I am no longer walking in fear and am committed to only walking by faith.

Peace and Blessings to you!

Keierra Reenell

# THANK YOU

I will like to firstly thank and give honor to my ABBA Father in Heaven. Thank You for giving me this gift and telling me it was time to share it with the world. Thank you to Dr. Groove for coming to Simeon High School and sharpening my gift. Thank you to DJ for making me go to all those open mics. Thank you, Mrs. Mary, for taking me to bind my first book in 5th grade at Kinkos. Thanks to Ms. Whaley for telling me I had great talent to write. Thank you, Shani, for calling me prolific! Thanks Mrs. Oleck, Mr. H, Mr. Yarch, Mrs. Parker-Barr, Mrs. Jones, Granny Mariah, Auntie Deborah and all the ones who know they impacted my life in some way shape or form. I am who I am today because of God's grace and your imprint in my heart so thank you. THANKS SO MUCH to Xulon Press and Mr. Jeff Fiztgerald for being persistent to send me those emails. I am a published author because of faith and your nudge. And lastly but certainly not least, thank you to all who are reading this book right now! This book would be nothing had you not taken the time to pick it up and open the pages. May the LORD bless you and keep you, and show you His salvation!

If you would like to contact me please follow me on Instagram @kei_reenell

CPSIA information can be obtained
at www.ICGtesting.com
Printed in the USA
LVHW011739190421
684916LV00016B/817